All About Sea Turtles

ALL ABOUT ANIMALS ★ IN THE SEA ★

Kerrily Sapet

EZ READERS
AN IMPRINT OF
MITCHELL LANE PUBLISHERS

CREATING YOUNG NONFICTION READERS

EZ Readers offer nonfiction for beginning readers in PreK through first grade, using simple language, clear illustrations, and engaging facts to build vocabulary and confidence.

TIPS FOR READING NONFICTION WITH BEGINNING READERS

Talk about Nonfiction

Begin by explaining that nonfiction books give us information that is true. The book will be organized around a specific topic or idea, and we may learn new facts through reading.

Look at the Parts

Most nonfiction books have helpful features. Our *EZ Readers* include color photographs and graphic aids, a table of contents, a glossary, and an index. Share the purpose of these features with your reader.

Color Photos and Graphic Aids

A lot of information can be found by "reading" photos, charts, maps, and other graphic aids found within nonfiction texts. Help your reader learn more about the different ways information can be displayed.

Table of Contents

Located at the front of the book, this list shows the big ideas within the text and the page numbers where they can be found.

Glossary

Located at the back of the book, the glossary defines key words and phrases that are related to the topic. These words and phrases can be found in the text in colored type.

Index

Located at the back of the book, an index is an alphabetical list of topics and the page numbers where they can be found.

With a little help and guidance about reading nonfiction, you can feel good about introducing a young reader to the world of *EZ Readers* nonfiction books.

EZ Readers is an imprint of:

Mitchell Lane PUBLISHERS

2001 SW 31st Avenue
Hallandale, FL 33009
mitchelllanepub.com

First Edition, 2026.

Author: Kerrily Sapet
Editor: Morgan Brody

ISBN 979-8-89260-840-4 (library binding)
ISBN 979-8-90145-039-0 (paperback)
ISBN 979-8-89260-942-5 (ebook)

LC record available at https://lccn.loc.gov/2025950880

Photo credits: Shutterstock, ROMAN RYBALKO, cover, 1; Shutterstock, Northern Owl, cover, 1, 2, 3, 4, 8, 15, 19; Shutterstock, Catherine Scotton, cover, 1; Adobe, 3, 9, 10, 14, 18; Shutterstock, Brocreative, 5; Shutterstock, Parilov, 6–7; Shutterstock, Dmitry Demkin, 9, 22; Shutterstock, Wirestock Creators, 10–11, 22; Shutterstock, Kjersti Joergensen, 12–13, 22; Shutterstock, Drew McArthur, 14; Shutterstock, seasoning_17, 18, 22; Shutterstock, Rich Carey, 20, 22; Shutterstock, woopics, 21

Table of Contents

Meeting An Ocean Swimmer

Imagine you are in a kayak. The sun shines. The water is warm.

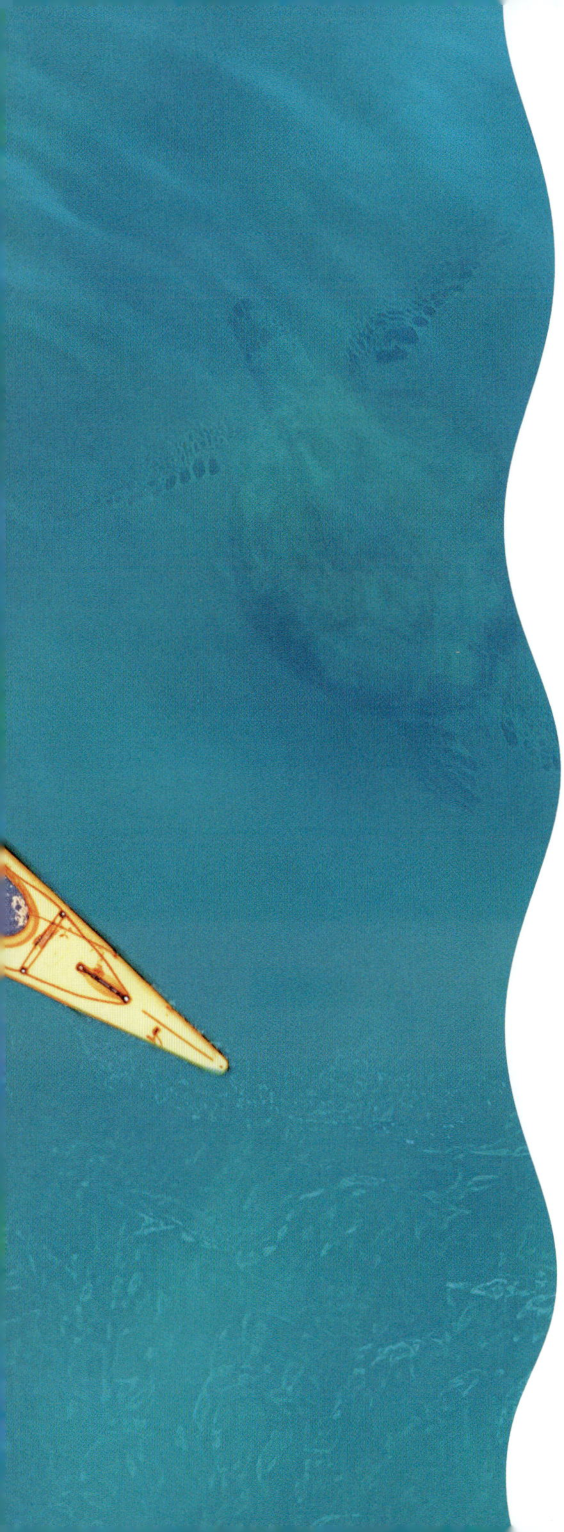

A large heart-shaped shell rises in the water. A head peeks out. A sea turtle! It's as long as a baseball bat and weighs as much as a refrigerator.

Turtle Watching

The sea turtle is reddish-brown. Its head sticks out of its bony shell. The scales on its shell are like armor. It swims with **flippers**.

TURTLE TRUTHS!

There are seven types of sea turtles. Some are the size of a dinner plate. Others are the size of a golf cart.

TURTLE TRUTHS!

Sea turtles can hold their breath for seven hours.

The turtle pokes its head above water. Sea turtles are not fish. They are **reptiles**. They breathe air, like you.

The turtle is quiet. Sea turtles chirp and grunt but people can't hear them. You see one turtle. They often swim alone. A group of sea turtles is called a flotilla.

TURTLE TRUTHS!

One type of sea turtle eats hundreds of jellyfish every day.

Looking for Food

Fish swim near your boat. The turtle doesn't eat them. Sea turtles eat seagrasses, crabs, and clams. Sea turtles don't have teeth. They have beaks like parrots that crush shells and cut food.

The turtle swims away.
Sea turtles **migrate**.
They swim across
oceans to find food.
They find the beaches
where they were born
to build nests.

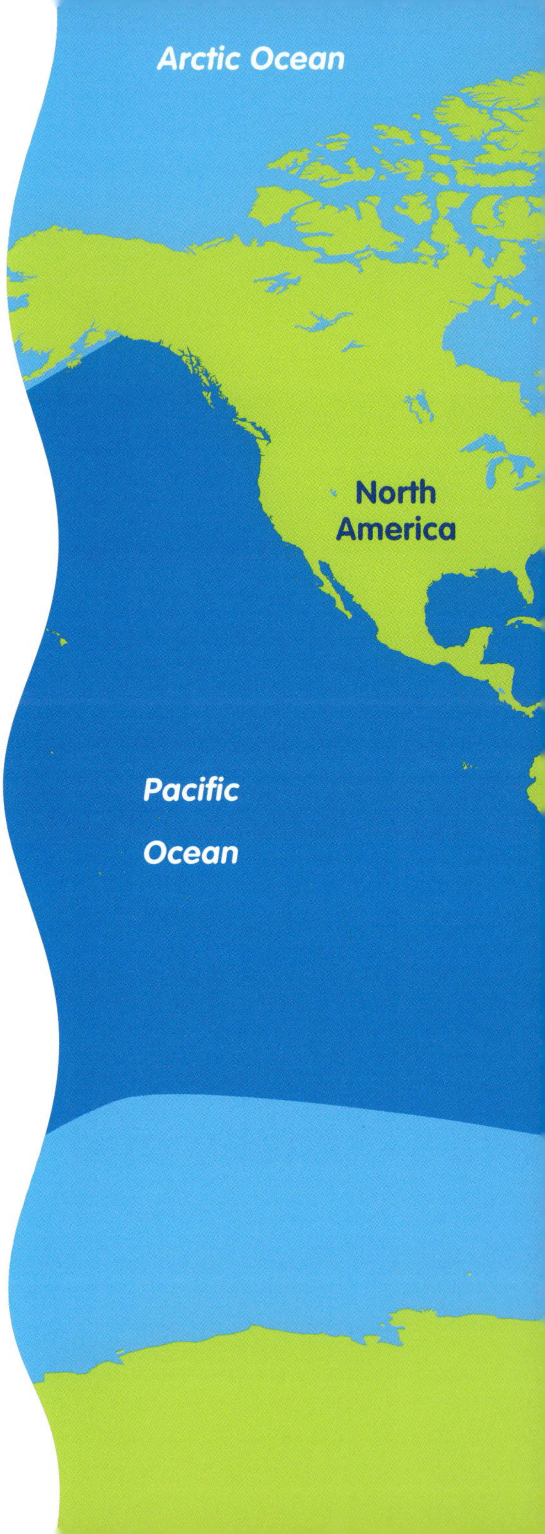

Where Do Sea Turtles Live?

TURTLE TRUTHS!

If the nest is warm, the **hatchlings** will be females. If it's cold, they will be males.

Sea Turtle Families and the Future

Sea turtles lay eggs that look like ping pong balls. Baby sea turtles are called hatchlings. They are as long as a paperclip and as heavy as a new pencil.

Sea turtles can live 70 years. Today, only a few sea turtles remain. **Pollution** harms them. Maybe someday you will see a real sea turtle!

Parts of a Sea Turtle

Glossary

flipper (FLIP-uhr)
a flat paddle on a sea turtle's side

hatchling (HA-ch-ling)
a baby sea turtle

migration (my-GRAY-shun)
when animals move to find food, warmer water, or home

pollution (po-LOO-shun)
dirty air, water, or land

reptile (REP-ti-ul) an animal that breathes air, has a backbone, scaly skin, and lays eggs on land

Quiz

1. **Are sea turtles fish?**

   A. Yes B. No

2. **Do sea turtles breathe air?**

   A. Yes B. No

3. **Do sea turtles eat sharks?**

   A. Yes B. No

4. **Are turtle babies called hatchlings?**

   A. Yes B. No

ANSWER KEY:
1. No
2. Yes
3. No
4. Yes

Further Reading

Arnold, Quinn. *Sea Turtles.* Mankato, MN: Creative Paperbacks, 2025.

Ellis, Elina. *But Where Do Sea Turtles Live?* Toronto, Ontario: Kids Can Press, 2025.

Moore, Lindsay. *Yoshi and the Ocean: A Sea Turtle's Incredible Journey Home.* New York, NY: Greenwillow Books, 2022.

On the Internet

Animals A to Z

https://www.montereybayaquarium.org/animals/animals-a-to-z/green-turtle

Meet the sea turtles living at the Monterrey Bay Aquarium.

Green Sea Turtles

https://kids.nationalgeographic.com/animals/reptiles/facts/green-sea-turtle

Read more and watch a video about sea turtles.

Sea Turtles

https://seaworld.org/animals/all-about/sea-turtles/

See pictures and learn about saving sea turtles.

Index

About the Author

Kerrily Sapet has written more than 30 books for kids. She lives near Chicago with her family. Sapet likes visiting a sea turtle named Nickel at the Shedd Aquarium. Nickel got her name because she swallowed a nickel in the ocean. Sapet saw a sea turtle laying eggs at night when she was in Florida. She hopes to see sea turtle hatchlings someday.